D0124335

Pebble® Plus

Understanding Differences

Some Kids Are Deaf

Revised Edition

Clinton Macomb
Public Library

by Lola M. Schaefer

CAPSTONE PRESS
a capstone imprint

Download the Capstone 4D app!

- Ask an adult to search in the Apple App Store or Google Play for "Capstone 4D".
- Click Install (Android) or Get, then Install (Apple).
- Open the app.
- Scan any of the following spreads with this icon:

When you scan a spread, you'll find fun extra stuff to go with this book! You can also find these things on the web at www.capstone4D.com using the password: **deaf.09977**

Pebble Plus is published by Capstone Press,
1710 Roe Crest Drive, North Mankato, Minnesota 56003
www.mycapstone.com

Copyright © 2018 by Capstone Press, a Capstone imprint.
All rights reserved. No part of this publication may be reproduced in whole or in part, or stored in a retrieval system, or transmitted in any form or by any means, electronic, mechanical, photocopying, recording, or otherwise, without written permission of the publisher.

Library of Congress Cataloging-in-Publication Data is available on the Library of Congress website.
ISBN 978-1-5435-0997-7 (library binding)
ISBN 978-1-5435-1001-0 (paperback)
ISBN 978-1-5435-1005-8 (ebook pdf)

Editorial Credits
Sarah Bennett, designer; Tracy Cummins, media researcher; Tori Abraham, production specialist

Photo Credits
Capstone: 12; Capstone Studio: Karon Dubke, 5, 9, 13, 15, 17, 19; Science Source: Life in View, 11, Spencer Grant, 7; Shutterstock: adriaticfoto, Cover, Andrey_Popov, 21, DoozyDo, Design Element

Note to Parents and Teachers

The Understanding Differences set supports national social studies standards related to individual development and identity. This book describes and illustrates children who are deaf. The images support early readers in understanding the text. The repetition of words and phrases helps early readers learn new words. This book also introduces early readers to subject-specific vocabulary words, which are defined in the Glossary section. Early readers may need assistance to read some words and to use the Table of Contents, Glossary, Read More, Internet Sites, Critical Thinking Questions, and Index sections of the book.

Printed in the United States of America.
010775S18

Table of Contents

Deafness 4
Tools for Hearing. 8
Talking. 12
Everyday Life 16
Glossary 22
Read More. 23
Internet Sites 23
Critical Thinking Questions 24
Index 24

Deafness

Some kids are deaf.
Kids who are deaf
cannot hear.

WHOA!
JUDY BLU

Some kids are born deaf.
Other kids become deaf
from a sickness
or from getting hurt.

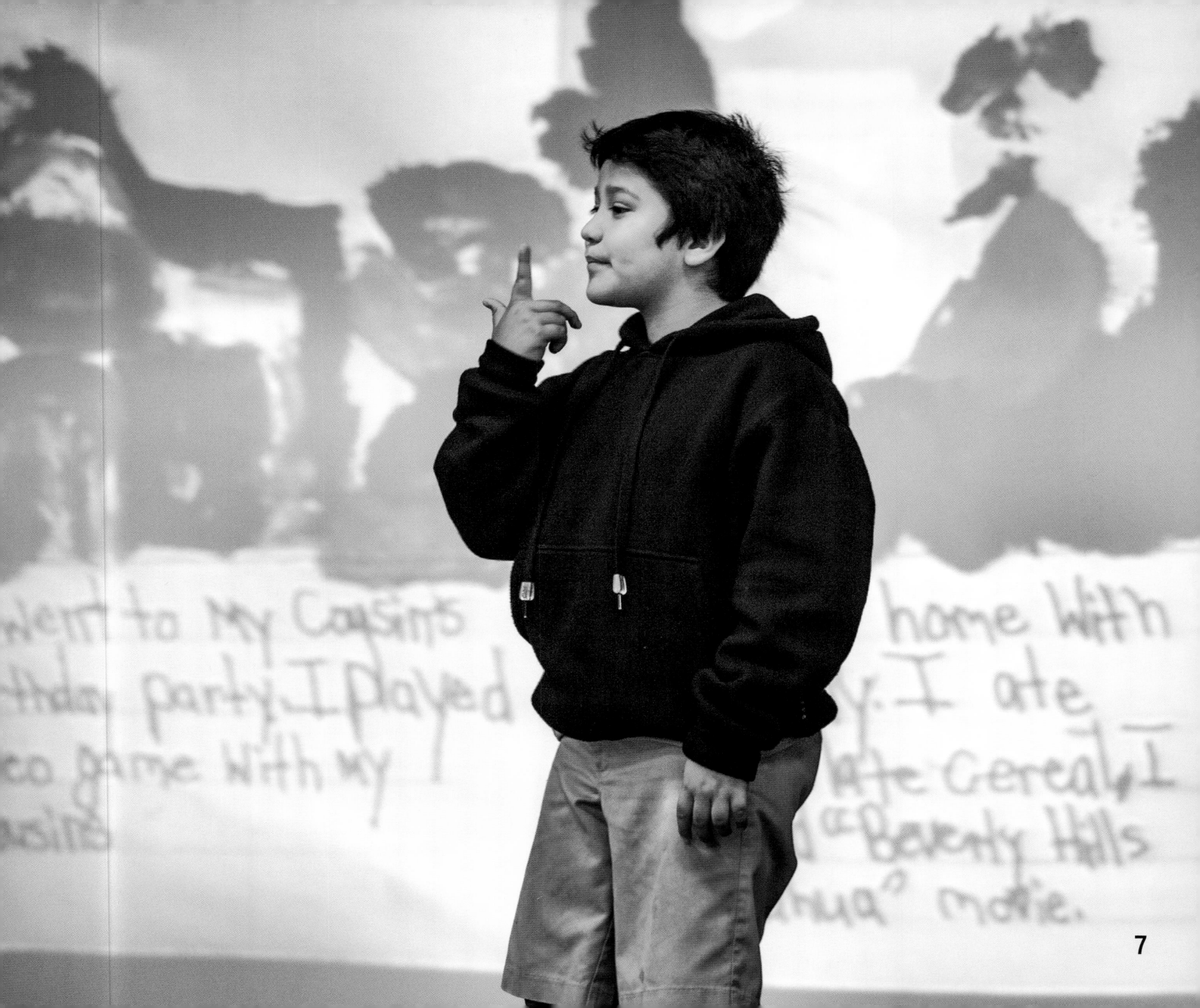
went to My Cousins
home With
party. I played
y. I ate
co game With my
ate Cereal. I
Beverly Hills
nua' movie.

Tools for Hearing

Some kids can hear a little.
They wear hearing aids
to hear sounds louder.

Some kids who are deaf
get cochlear implants.
Implants help them hear
some sounds.

Talking

Some kids who are deaf use sign language to talk. Sign language is hand signs that stand for letters, words, and numbers.

Sign Language

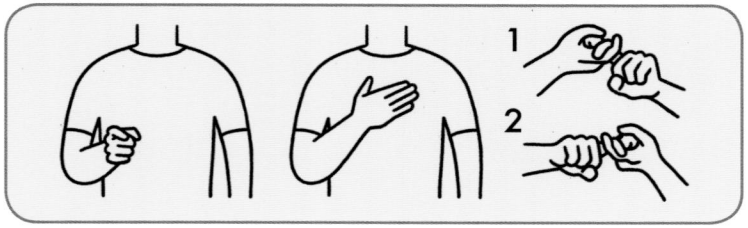

You are my friend.

BRAIN TEASER!
Level A
Morgan
Melissa
Aisha
Cullen
Taylor
punctuation bingo
addition
TELL-TIME
28

Some kids who are deaf use their voice to talk. Speech therapists teach them to speak clearly.

Artic Photos
TH

Everyday Life

Kids who are deaf depend
on their sense of sight.
Flashing lights tell them
it's time for class.

Kids who are deaf watch TV
with closed captioning.
The words tell what people
on TV are saying.

TV
G
MACAPA
AMAZON
BASIN
BRAZIL
STRADDLING THE EQUATOR,
MACAPA, BRAZIL IS AN EXOTIC WORLD
ORION
MTS STEREO

Kids who are deaf depend on their sense of touch. They can feel a phone vibrate when a friend sends a text message.

14:23
97%
Maria
Hey! What's up?
Not much. Can you hang out?
Sure, I'll ask my dad.
OK, let's bike to the park.
Sure! See you soon.
Send

Glossary

cochlear implant—a small electronic device that is surgically put into a person's head; cochlear implants allow sounds to get to the brain

deaf—being unable to hear

hearing aid—a small electronic device that people wear in or behind one or both ears; hearing aids make sounds louder

senses—ways of learning about your surroundings; hearing, smelling, touching, tasting, and sight are the five senses

sign language—hand signs that stand for words, letters, and numbers

speech therapist—a person who is trained to help people learn to speak clearly

text message—words sent from a cell phone to another person's cell phone

Read More

Clay, Kathryn. *Signing in My World: Sign Language for Kids.* Time to Sign. North Mankato, Minn.: Capstone, 2014.

Kent, Deborah. *What Is It Like to Be Deaf?* Overcoming Barriers. Berkeley Heights, N.J.: Enslow Elementary, 2012.

Internet Sites

Use FactHound to find Internet sites related to this book.

Visit *www.facthound.com*

Just type **9781543509977** and go.

Critical Thinking Questions

1. What other senses are helpful to a person who is deaf?

2. Describe sign language.

3. How do flashing lights at school help children who are deaf?

Index

closed captioning, 18
cochlear implants, 10
flashing lights, 16
friends, 20
hear, 4, 8
hearing aids, 8
sickness, 6
sight, 16
sign language, 12
sounds, 8, 10
speech therapist, 14
talking, 12, 14
touch, 20
TV, 18
voice, 14